The In-Fisherman Secrets Series

W9-COJ-498

THIRTY TIME-TESTED TIPS FOR
FRESHWATER FISHING

**from the Editors of
In-Fisherman Magazine**

Published by
In-Fisherman® Inc.

The In-Fisherman Secrets Series

THIRTY TIME-TESTED TIPS FOR
FRESHWATER FISHING

Publisher *Stuart Legaard*
Editor In Chief *Doug Stange*
Editors *Dave Csanda, Steve Hoffman,*
Steve Quinn, Matt Straw
Director *Al Lindner*
Project Coordinator *Scott Lawrence*
Copy Editor *Joann Phipps*
Photo Editor/Design *Jan Finger*
Layout & Design *Jim Pfaff with Scott Lawrence*

ISBN 0-929384-94-6
The In-Fisherman Secrets Series
An
F (Fish) + **L** (Location) + **P** (Presentation) = **S** (Success)™
Educational Service

First Edition, 1998

TABLE OF CONTENTS

INTRODUCTION

Some anglers always seem to catch fish. These anglers are always a new technique or two or a new bait or two ahead of the rest. When the hordes toss spinners and spoons, this bunch works plastics. When everyone else fishes during the day, they fish at night. When the fishing pressure is on weedbeds, they move to rocks, or look deeper, or move to open water. And when they can't move, can't escape the crowd, they use finesse techniques where standard techniques are the norm; or they modify a standard technique when finesse is the norm. A new bait, a new technique, an old standard modified. A fake here, a sleight of hand there. Understanding when to zig instead of zag is part of the process, part of what In-Fisherman is about.

Fishing is a break, a chance to get away from it all and escape the hustle and bustle of the workaday world. But most anglers also want to catch fish, and it is this part of the process that In-Fisherman has addressed for more than 25 years.

We are about teaching anglers how to catch more fish. The thrill of fishing is in the pursuit, the challenge of getting to know the characteristics of each fish species, in order to make judgments about where to find them and how to catch them.

Thirty Time-Tested Tips For Freshwater Fishing is gleaned from thousands of in-depth articles featured over the years in *In-Fisherman* magazine.

How to use this book—Each tip follows a format that includes a short introduction, capturing the essence of the event, followed by tackle recommendations to help you fish efficiently. Seasonal icons suggest the seasons during which a tip applies—spring 🍂 , summer ☀ , fall 🍁 , winter ❄ . And finally, a technical section addresses details about location (finding fish) and presentation (getting them to bite). Illustrations that accompany each tip result from thousands of hours of pleasant research.

Welcome to a small part of the world of In-Fisherman. For more about fishing, contact us at In-Fisherman, In-Fisherman Dr., Brainerd, MN 56425. Or visit us on the Internet at <www.in-fisherman.com>.

Doug Stange
Editor In Chief

BOTTOM BUMPING BLADES FOR LARGEMOUTHS

For 20 years, anglers have been catching limits of bass by burning spinnerbaits a few inches below the surface. Times have changed, however, and bass have changed. Sadly, the new breed of fish often seems burnt out on the speedy flash of a steadily retrieved spinnerbait. Instead, anglers are working spinnerbaits near or on the bottom in water 5 to 25 feet deep. Deep and slow may be one of the most effective spinnerbait presentations ever devised for largemouth in lakes, rivers, and reservoirs.

When

Tackle

Rod: 6- to 7-foot medium-heavy-power casting rod. *Reel:* slow- to moderate-speed baitcasting reel. *Line:* 17- or 20-pound-test abrasion-resistant mono.

Rigging

Early practitioners of slow rollin' used 1/2- to 1-ounce spinnerbaits with a small Colorado blade and a moderate to large willow-leaf blade. Lure manufacturers have listened to the advice of their pro staffs to refine blade combinations and to offer new styles. New models, designed specifically for bottom-bouncing techniques, incorporate more lead for a straighter drop and smaller blades to keep the bait deep.

Versatile 5/8- to 1-ounce spinnerbaits with tandem Colorado, Willow-leaf, and Indiana blades are used for slow rollin' and dead draggin' presentations. Substitute a single-bladed Colorado or Indiana model for the deepest slow rollin' presentations.

Slow roll a spinnerbait by making a long cast over a substantial stretch of bass-holding cover, then retrieving just fast enough for the bait to tick the top of the cover. As the lure contacts weeds or wood, the blades change cadence, causing a change in vibration frequency and a sudden flash. To trigger bass that may be following the lure, give your reel a quick crank to make the bait jump away from cover. Adjust retrieve speed, lure weight, and blade design to keep the spinnerbait working near cover.

To dead drag a spinnerbait, make a long cast with a heavy spinnerbait, letting it fall on a free line to the target area. Then work the bait along the bottom with the rod tip, experimenting with movements as you would a jig, worm, or Carolina rig. When the spinnerbait reaches a drop, it flutters down and lands. Drag it up grades or over stumps, as the spinner arm deflects snags. Unlike slow rollin', the object is to maintain constant contact with the bottom. □

Slow Rollin'

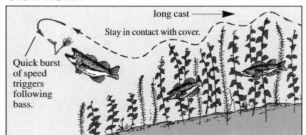

long cast

Stay in contact with cover.

Quick burst of speed triggers following bass.

Slow rollin' works any time bass are holding in short vegetation or near the tops of tall weeds or submerged trees or brush.

Dead Draggin'

Stay in contact with bottom.

Dead draggin' is most effective when bass are holding near the transition from weeds to a rock or clean sand bottom.

FINDING THE FIRST BASS OF SPRING

Largemouth bass return to the shallows during the brief transition period between the end of the cold-water season and the beginning of spring. The frigid water warms just enough to release bass from their winter sanctuaries. But these fish, seemingly afraid of their own shadows, are no easy catch.

When

Tackle

Rod: 6½- to 7-foot spinning rod. *Reel:* spinning reel with a long-cast spool. *Line:* 8- or 10-pound-test limp mono.

Reservoirs

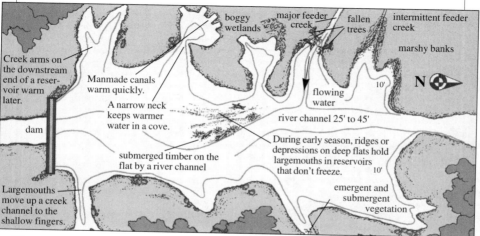

boggy wetlands

major feeder creek

fallen trees

intermittent feeder creek

marshy banks

Creek arms on the downstream end of a reservoir warm later.

Manmade canals warm quickly.

A narrow neck keeps warmer water in a cove.

dam

flowing water

river channel 25' to 45'

10'

N

submerged timber on the flat by a river channel

During early season, ridges or depressions on deep flats hold largemouths in reservoirs that don't freeze. 10'

Largemouths move up a creek channel to the shallow fingers.

emergent and submergent vegetation

Rigging

Baits for early season should be small and subtle. Rig a 3-inch tube bait or 4-inch plastic worm on a light-wire hook and small bullet sinker or a 1/16-ounce jig-head. Keep hook points needle sharp to ensure a solid hookset with light tackle.

Location

Bass in lakes move into backwaters as soon as the ice leaves. But not all bays are created equal. Bass often hold in less than a foot of water, though some of the water in the bay should be at least 3 feet deep to provide sanctuary from predators and changing water temperatures. Since northwest winds are prevalent during spring, bays on the northwest side of the lake tend to warm first. Bays with a broad mouth also warm quickly, but lose their warmth if shifting winds push the surface layer into the main lake. Bays separated from the lake by a narrow channel retain their warmth from day to day and often hold more bass.

Some reservoirs offer the same features that draw ice-out bass in lakes. The upstream end of an impoundment is usually shallower and subject to higher flows, so ice leaves earlier. Creek arms with little running water, especially those oriented in a northwesterly direction, also warm faster than main-reservoir areas. Bass move into the dead grass in these areas and behave much like fish in natural lakes. Fallen trees and other shoreline cover may look attractive, but in most sections of the reservoir, they lie in water too deep and too cold to attract bass early in the season. ☐

Lakes

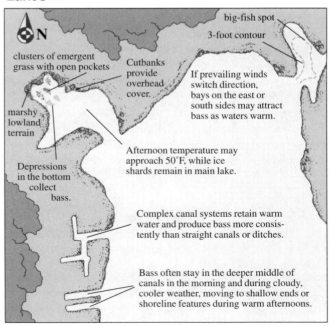

N

big-fish spot

3-foot contour

clusters of emergent grass with open pockets

Cutbanks provide overhead cover.

If prevailing winds switch direction, bays on the east or south sides may attract bass as waters warm.

marshy lowland terrain

Depressions in the bottom collect bass.

Afternoon temperature may approach 50°F, while ice shards remain in main lake.

Complex canal systems retain warm water and produce bass more consistently than straight canals or ditches.

Bass often stay in the deeper middle of canals in the morning and during cloudy, cooler weather, moving to shallow ends or shoreline features during warm afternoons.

SHALLOW CRANKBAITS FOR LARGEMOUTH BASS

A peek into the crankbait box of nearly every top bass pro reveals a set of shallow-running crankbaits. This category of baits includes the Bomber 2A, Manns 1-Minus, Luhr-Jensen Speed Trap, Reef Runner Scooter, and similar-shape baits that run a maximum of 2 or 3 feet deep. To find fish or to trigger them in shallow water, these fast-vibrating baits excel over spinnerbaits, buzzbaits, or topwaters.

When

Tackle

Rod: 6½-foot casting rod. *Reel:* high-speed baitcasting reel. *Line:* 17- or 20-pound-test mono.

Rigging

Shallow-running crankbaits are designed to cover water fast and draw strikes from fish that may refuse to bite a lure moving at a slower pace. Fish faced with a quick decision to strike or to let a potential meal pass often choose to strike. Mann's 1-Minus and Baby 1-Minus are unique, running less than a foot deep and exhibiting a wide wobble. These attributes are well suited for covering flats when weeds grow toward the surface in early summer.

In rocky cover, a Bomber 2A or Reef Runner Scooter bangs off boulders and careens off ledges, irresistible to bass holding there. These short-billed baits run horizontally and hang up less than divers with extended bills. When they deflect off rocks and

turn sideways, bass can't resist them. They're great in rivers, too, for largemouth and smallmouth bass.

Location

In southeastern reservoirs, water levels typically rise in spring, following a fall and winter drawdown. Largemouths roam the inside weededge prior to spawning and also spread across weedy flats. Remember that spawning in a reservoir may extend over several months, depending on lake characteristics and weather conditions. Groups of bass may be in prespawn, while others are actively spawning, and some have already spawned.

Presentation

Make long casts over submergent weedgrowth to cover more water when searching for active fish. Heavy line causes the bait to run even shallower, and its strength is needed when a big fish burrows into thick cover. A high-speed reel also helps retrieve lures quickly, triggering savage strikes from active fish. Try to run the lure so it just ticks the top of the grass or runs close by patches of vegetation. □

Burnin' The Flats

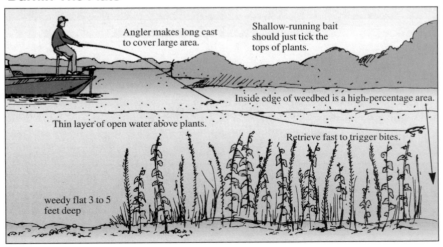

13

CATCHING BASS ON THE INSIDE EDGE

Since the advent of structure fishing, many bass anglers have considered deeper better for finding groups of big bass, at least in the absence of shallow cover like fallen trees, stumps, lily pads, and boat docks. The section of water between the bank and brush, stumps, or weedbeds doesn't look productive, but looks are deceiving. During the first few months of bass season, the inside edge is the focus of much largemouth bass activity. Bass use the shallow edge to find and corner prey and to build spawning beds that escape the view of most bass anglers.

When

Tackle

Rod: 6- to 7-foot medium-power spinning or casting rod. *Reel:* medium-capacity spinning or baitcasting reel. *Line:* 10- to 14-pound mono.

Rigging

An array of baits are effective for largemouths holding along inside edges. Lightly weighted or unweighted soft plastics land softly and fall slowly, attributes that work well for spawning fish, or wary bass in clear water. Crankbaits and Carolina rigs work along deeper inside edges and allow for fast searching for groups of fish. Spinnerbaits are versatile in terms of depth, but work best in stained water. Try topwaters once water temperature rises into the 60°F range.

Presentation

In a way, inside edges are easy to fish because patterns are shallow and most targets are visible. The flip side is that bass tend to be wary, and approaching anglers are easily visible. In water less than 5 feet deep, start with a 6-inch soft plastic stickbait worked parallel to the edge or cast it into pockets in the weeds. Twitch it slowly if bass are active or cruising. When the fish are bedding or when they're less active, make long casts and let the bait settle.

Tube baits are another top choice for these conditions. They offer a soft landing and lifelike action. When rigged with a pegged bullet weight and nudged along the bottom with occasional hops, they resemble small crawfish or minnows nuzzling into the bottom. Tubes with a light insert weight or weighted hook glide like baitfish. This presentation takes fish under the toughest conditions. Light jig-n-pigs and plastic worms or lizards also are fine for pitching into pockets.

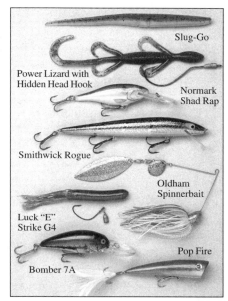

Slug-Go

Power Lizard with Hidden Head Hook

Normark Shad Rap

Smithwick Rogue

Oldham Spinnerbait

Luck "E" Strike G4

Pop Fire

Bomber 7A

At times, though, floating minnowbaits like the Normark Rapala, Smithwick Rouge, or A.C. Shiner draw the most strikes. Slow twitches interspersed with pauses work around spawning time time or when bass hold in weed or brush pockets. And don't neglect topwaters, which can be cast far and worked in countless patterns in shallow conditions. Poppers work well during early summer, once spawning is over. □

Fishing The Edge

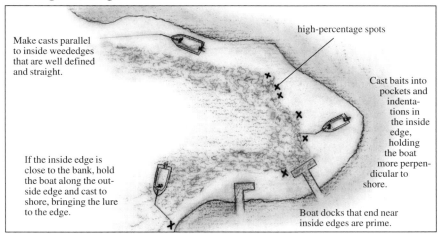

Make casts parallel to inside weededges that are well defined and straight.

high-percentage spots

Cast baits into pockets and indentations in the inside edge, holding the boat more perpendicular to shore.

If the inside edge is close to the bank, hold the boat along the outside edge and cast to shore, bringing the lure to the edge.

Boat docks that end near inside edges are prime.

15

FINDING FALL LARGEMOUTHS IN RIVERS

Largemouth bass don't like current. Oh, they take advantage of the way it concentrates baitfish, and they instinctively know how to hold behind structure and rush out to catch prey passing upstream or downstream in rivers. But for three seasons of the year, they tend to avoid it. The largemouth's aversion to flowing water begins in midfall when they undertake major migrations to spots that shelter them from current.

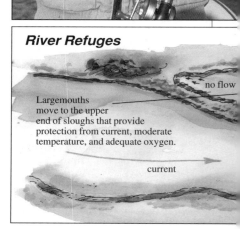

When

Tackle

Rod: 6- to 7-foot medium-power casting or spinning rod. *Reel:* medium-capacity baitcasting or spinning reel. *Line:* 12- or 14-pound mono.

River Refuges

no flow

Largemouths move to the upper end of sloughs that provide protection from current, moderate temperature, and adequate oxygen.

current

Location

Tracking studies on several major rivers demonstrate that largemouths instinctively seek somewhat deeper and protected areas that also provide sufficient oxygen. In some cases, largemouths migrate before conditions get tough, as early as mid-September in some areas. In other systems, they remain, dipping into side channels or backwaters later, until water temperatures falling into the low 50°F range boot them to their wintering areas.

While the timing may vary, the move's essential. In fall, finding these winter refuges can provide a bonanza. Refuges are not abundant, however, and it's not always obvious why bass choose certain areas, shunning what appear to be equally suitable ones. A typical 10-mile stretch of river may contain only a handful of prime wintering locations. Bass typically favor the upper ends of deeper sloughs, protected sections of tributaries, and manmade harbors.

Catch & Release

Catch-and-immediate-release fishing should be the rule on major rivers in fall. The popularity of fall tournaments on the Hudson River has apparently led to declines in the largemouth bass population. Anglers have pulled limits from wintering areas as late as November and have transported them 25 miles or more to a weigh-in site. While the homing instinct might or might not guide a bass back to its chosen site, it may not have the energy to survive the winter.

Presentation

Bass in river sanctuaries usually aren't deep, and moderate levels of catch-and-release fishing shouldn't harm populations. In early fall, spinnerbaits and crankbaits take fish, along with jigs, worms, and other standard presentations. As water temperatures fall into the 40°F range, grubs, finesse worms, and hair jigs become more effective. During ice cover, anglers continue to take bass on tip-ups baited with shiners, or on small jigging spoons and tiny ice flies tipped with maggots. □

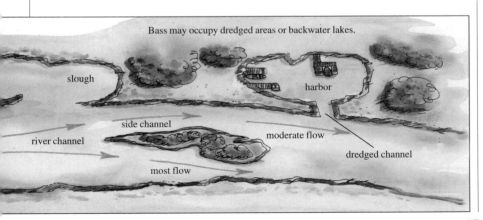

Bass may occupy dredged areas or backwater lakes.

slough

harbor

side channel

moderate flow

river channel

dredged channel

most flow

HAIR JIGS FOR SMALLMOUTHS

Soft plastic baits in every conceivable color have displaced hair jigs in the tackle boxes of most smallmouth bass anglers. Soft plastics are widely available and catch smallmouth everywhere they swim. But well-tied hair jigs possess a solid profile, range of textures, and subtle breathing movement that plastic baits can't match. They remain one of the most versatile and effective lures for smallmouths in rivers, lakes, and reservoirs.

When

Tackle

Rod: 6½- to 7½-foot medium-power fast-action spinning rod. *Reel:* medium-capacity spinning reel. *Line:* 6- to 10-pound-test mono.

Presentation

In lakes, use minnow-imitating jigs on shallow flats, deep flats, or along the edge or rock bars. Cast and stop the jig just above the water, letting it drop on a fairly tight line, with the rod tip dropping to 9 o'clock. As the jig ticks bottom, lift the rod toward 11 o'clock, pause, and follow it back to bottom. Vary the speed of the retrieve and the speed of the lift, depending on the mood of the fish.

To imitate crayfish, use a brown or black pattern with a small, thin strip of pork, like one leg from an Uncle Josh U-2 pork eel. Crawl the jig across rocks and gravel. Or hop or bounce it. Slowly raise the rod tip from 9 to 11 o'clock and reel in slack line as you move the tip back down to 9 o'clock. Some anglers prefer to move the rod parallel to the water, which offers less opportunity to lift the jig off the bottom. □

Basic Swimming Retrieve

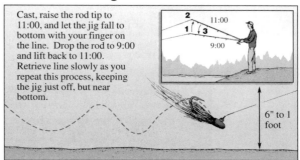

Basic Dragging Retrieve

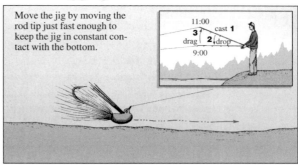

Where different head styles perform best (top to bottom).

Arky-style head (wood)—*Deener's Jigs & Things Fox Hair Jig*
Standup-style head (gravel and scattered rock)—*Bull Dog Hair Jig*
Football head (gravel and scattered rock)—*Ray Price Finesse Jig*
Aspirin head (broken rock or boulders)—*Bass 'N Bait Snakie*
Maxie Bullet head (swimming retrieves)—*Bert's Threadfin Shad*
Eye-in-nose bullet head (weeds)—*Andy's Penetrator*

LIVEBAIT TACTICS FOR SMALLMOUTHS

When smallmouths are in a neutral or negative feeding mood, a slow presentation rather than a rapid retrieve produces more and bigger fish—even though a fast presentation covers more water. Livebait is presented slowly, but also possesses the added triggering power of natural scent, profile, and action. Live baits also can be presented more effectively in deeper water—where inactive fish are more likely found—than crankbaits and other artificials. Livebait should be an option whenever you face tough conditions.

When

Tackle

Rod: 6½- to 7-foot medium-power spinning rod with a moderately fast action. *Reel:* spinning reel with a long-cast spool. *Line:* 6- to 8-pound-test limp mono.

Rigging

When smallmouths are in water shallower than 10 feet, pinch on enough lead shot a foot above your hook to slowly sink the bait. For deeper water, slip a walking sinker or bell sinker on your line and tie on a #10 barrel swivel. Attach a 2- to

4-foot length of 6- or 8-pound-test monofilament leader to the other end of the swivel. Use a #2 or #4 hook for minnows like shiners and chubs, and a #6 or #8 hook for crawlers and leeches.

Presentation

Cast smoothly to avoid tearing the bait off the hook, and let it sink to the bottom. Retrieve slack line and slowly lift the rod tip from 9 to 11 o'clock, dragging the sinker across the bottom. Pause to let the bait wiggle enticingly, reel in any slack line as you drop the rod back to 9 o'clock, then move the sinker forward again. When you feel a fish take the bait, follow it with your rod tip as you tighten the line. Then set the hook.

When searching for fish, backtroll with a slip-sinker rig along a breakline or the edge of a bar. Keep your bait almost vertical and pause frequently to let it work. With an open bail and your finger pinching the line tight to your rod, you'll be able to feed line to a smallmouth that grabs the bait and moves off quickly. When you find fish, anchor and cast to cover the area. □

Sinker Weight By Depth

Depth	Recommended Sinker Weight	Distance From Boat
15' or less	1/8 or 1/4 oz.	45' to 60'
15' to 25'	1/4 or 3/8 oz.	30' to 60'
25' to 45'	3/8 to 1/2 oz.	beneath boat
beyond 45'	3/4 oz.	beneath boat

Slip Sinker Rigging

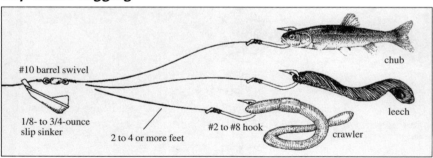

#10 barrel swivel

1/8- to 3/4-ounce slip sinker

2 to 4 or more feet

#2 to #8 hook

chub

leech

crawler

SMALL JIGS FOR BIG SMALLMOUTHS

Inactive smallmouths seldom pursue large lures, but a small, unobtrusive bait is another matter. Tiny jigs, for example, often are hit (out of reflex?) by fish that would refuse a larger offering. What's more, the places where inactive smallmouths tend to gather following a cold front or other drastic change often are the same year after year. So, small jigs just make sense for smallmouths.

When

Tackle

Rod: 7½-foot medium-light-power spinning rod. *Reel:* medium-capacity spinning reel with a long-cast spool. *Line:* 6-pound-test limp mono.

Rigging

Under tough conditions, start with a 1/16-ounce jighead with a light wire #2 or #4 hook. Run a 1- to 2-inch plastic tube or grub body against the head. On windy days, try the same plastic bodies on a slightly heavier jig, up to 1/8 ounce. The whole package should be black, brown, or some other natural color—unless the water's cloudy, in which case a splash or orange of chartreuse on the head or tail helps bass find it.

Location

As Small As Peanuts

1/16-ounce Gopher Mushroom Head with 2-inch Creme tube

homemade marabou jig

1/16-ounce Mushroom Head with 2-inch Berkley Micro Tube

3/32-ounce Mushroom with "bitten off" Berkley Ribbon Tail

3/32-ounce Mushroom with 2-inch Berkley Power Grub

Inactive smallmouths typically dump into 8 to 15 feet of water off classic bars, humps, and sunken islands, usually collecting on inside turns. After cold fronts, smallmouths hunker down in corners and other specific sections of a structural element. It's necessary to finesse the bait to get it in front of them, which means moving it slowly, which often is difficult during adverse weather.

Look for something different on inside turns that might attract the most fish, like a pile of boulders running down the edge of a bar in 10 to 12 feet of water. Another classic spot is the sharpest drop-off from the structure. A sheer wall that drops down to a sand basin at the base of a steep rock slide is a prime area. The more severe the cold front, the more fish funnel into these areas.

Presentation

Position the boat in deeper water adjacent to the inside turn where inactive smallies are likely holding. Make a long cast, let the jig sink, then begin a swimming retrieve. Hold the rod tip low during the drop, especially in strong wind. Lightweight jigs seldom touch bottom, and if they do, it's usually difficult to feel bottom because the jig touches down so slowly. Don't hop or rip the jig or make any other aggressive movements. Just drag, glide, or swim it through prime areas. □

Finding Inactive Smallmouths

In summer, active smallmouths use the tops of humps and rockbars, feeding heavily in 4 to 6 feet of water. Inactive smallmouths drop into deeper water. Inside turns such as *Areas A* and *B* will collect most of these bass after a cold front. Smallmouths may also gravitate toward the end of submerged points *(Area C)*, spreading out along transitions from rock to sand.

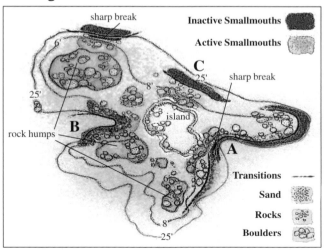

23

FINDING AND CATCHING RIVER SMALLMOUTHS DURING SPRING

During spring, river small-mouths have always posed something of a mystery. Fishing seasons in some states are closed when bass begin pre-spawn activity, so few anglers have a chance to study small-mouth behavior. Migratory patterns are easier to observe in southern waters lacking ice cover, where warmer tempera-tures and open seasons allow fishermen to follow smallmouths all year. Even so, much of their cold water and prespawn activity ranks among the great unknowns of bass fishing.

When

Tackle

Rod: 6½- to 7-foot medium-power cast-ing rod. *Reel:* medium-capacity bait-casting reel. *Line:* 10-pound-test mono.

Location

Water level usually is higher and dirtier in spring than during the rest of the year, producing stronger current, less visibility, and more submerged cover. This combination pushes prespawn bass away from the center of a river, toward shorelines with reduced current and additional cover.

Bait Options

Smallmouths often select nesting areas of mixed sand, gravel, and small rock, out of current flow and generally in water less than three feet deep. Pure sand is undesirable unless fish can sweep away a top layer, exposing a gravel base below. Proper spawning bottom with a thin coating of darker silt reduces visibility.

Large slack areas may draw huge numbers of prespawn bass. They may spread out across the slack area at low water, then tuck tighter to the bank if water levels rise, forcing them toward and along the downstream shoreline. Smaller slack water areas like those on the back sides of wing dams may only attract a few fish.

Subsurface baits usually work best for river smallmouths during spring. Shallow crankbaits in crayfish patterns, 1/8- or 1/4-ounce spinnerbaits, and #2 straight-shaft spinners are fine options.

Presentation

Early spring presentations for river bass should be geared to cover water fairly quickly, since determining location is the biggest key to success. Yet lures must not be so large and loud as to spook bass from biting. Think "subtle quickness" for scouting, with the option to switch to "subtle secondary" once key locations are determined.

Crankbaits and spinnerbaits are ideal for quickly scouting potential stretches of riverbank, island tailouts, large shallow eddies, and flooded cover. In general, cranks work best for open water where cover is limited to boulders, stumps, or scattered timber. Spinnerbaits are better choices for penetrating abundant cover like brush, weeds, or fallen trees. □

Primary And Secondary Locations

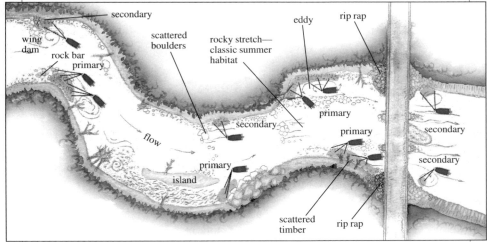

25

SUSPENDED SMALLMOUTHS

Smallmouths often suspend in pursuit of open-water baitfish like shad, alewives, smelt, ciscoes, trout, and emerald shiners. This seemingly illusive pattern occurs in an array of watersheds, from the mountain lakes of New Hampshire to the reservoirs of Utah and Nevada, and from the shield lakes of Canada to the huge impoundments of Texas and Tennessee. A wave of red-hot open-water patterns also occurs on the Great Lakes, where bass sometimes chase smelt, alewives, ciscoes and, at times, trout and shad.

When

Tackle

Rod: 6- to 7-foot medium-power spinning rod. *Reel:* medium-capacity spinning reel. *Line:* 8- to 12-pound-test mono.

Location

Smallmouths spawn at surface temperatures of about 64°F, during April, May, or June, depending on latitude. In some bodies of water, after spawning, as surface temperatures rise above 65°F in the shallows, groups of bass begin to suspend. Usually they move just off classic smallmouth structure. The typical zone of suspension may be from 5 to 30 feet down. Depth and timing depend on the type of forage. Within a few weeks of spawning, though, many smallmouths are drawn into open water.

Presentation

Scan open-water areas adjacent to classic structural elements that attract smallmouths. Early and late in the day, look for surface activity. Otherwise, search with electronics, looking for schools of bait. Sometimes it's possible to spot bigger fish—smallmouths or other predators—holding nearby. Bass and baitfish up high usually don't appear on sonar, but peering into the swells with polarized glasses might reveal the glittering sides of baitfish.

When smallmouths are breaking the surface, any darting surface bait may work. Or try a suspending minnowbait fished with a series of quick jerks as you quickly retrieve. As the morning wears on, track the fish by counting down a white or shad-colored grub on a 1/8-ounce ballhead jig. Vertical techniques with jigging spoons and swimming lures also can be productive when smallmouths hold in groups under clouds of baitfish. Drop swimming lures down to the level of the fish and use a lift-drop-hold presentation. □

Heddon Zara Spook

Buddha Baits Popfire

Charlie Nuchols Float 'n' Fly

Owner Ultrahead

Bill Lewis Rattle Trap

Thill Stealth Float

Kalin Hologram Tail

Normark H12 Husky Jerk

Smithwick Rattlin' Rogue

Nichols Pulsator

Norman Little "N"

Gremlin Rubbercor (rubber removed)

Rebel Spoonbill

Normark Shad Rap

Storm Deep ThunderStick Jr.

Normark Jigging Rapala

Hopkins Spoon

Bass'N Bait Rattle Snakie

Luhr-Jensen Crippled Herring

Smallmouths In Suspense

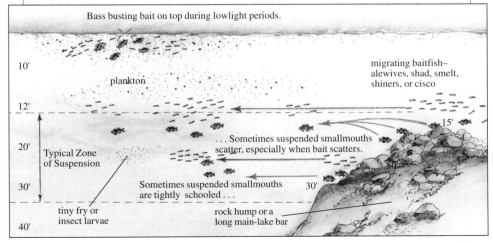

Bass busting bait on top during lowlight periods.

10'

plankton

migrating baitfish–
alewives, shad, smelt, shiners, or cisco

12'

15'

20'

Typical Zone of Suspension

...Sometimes suspended smallmouths scatter, especially when bait scatters.

50'

30'

Sometimes suspended smallmouths are tightly schooled...

30'

tiny fry or insect larvae

rock hump or a long main-lake bar

40'

27

JIGGING FOR WINTER WALLEYES

Catching more walleyes through the ice is as easy as one-two-three. With three basic jig styles, you can match your offering to the activity level of the fish. From least to most aggressive, the jig types include bare-bones leadhead jigs tipped with minnows, flash lures like the Bay De Noc Swedish Pimple and Acme Kastmaster spoons, and swimming lures like the Normark Jigging Rapala. Use these three lures and a few basic guidelines, singly or in some combination, to catch walleyes throughout the frozen-water season.

When

General Level of Winter Aggressiveness	Basic Jig Type
Aggressive	Swimming Lure (Jigging Rapala or Nils Master Jigger)
Moderately Aggressive	Flash Lure (Kastmaster or Swedish Pimple)
Not-So-Aggressive	Bare-Bones Leadhead Jig With Reversed Minnow

28

Tackle

Rod: 28- to 36-inch medium-heavy-power ice rod with a fast action. *Reel:* spinning reel with a medium-diameter spool and a smooth drag. *Line:* 8- to 12-pound-test mono.

Rigging

For less-active fish, select a plain leadhead jig just large enough to control the minnow—usually 1/16- to 1/4-ounce. Insert the hook just behind and parallel to the the dorsal fin of a 3- to 5-inch minnow. Swimming and flash lures should be attached to the line with a snap or split ring. Tip treble hooks with a minnow head.

Presentation

All three jig styles are presented in the same way—just add more snap and movement with aggressive lure styles to trigger active fish. Begin with the bait 3 to 9 inches off the bottom and lift the bait 1½ to 3 feet. Immediately return the rod tip to the starting position, allowing the bait to swim, flutter, or fall on a slack line. Pause several seconds before repeating, or jiggle the bait in place by subtly moving the rod tip up and down 1/16 inch. The movement, flash, and vibration of the bait attracts, while the return and pause triggers. □

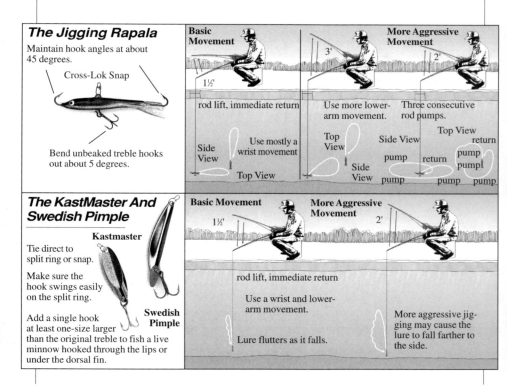

The Jigging Rapala

Maintain hook angles at about 45 degrees.

Cross-Lok Snap

Bend unbeaked treble hooks out about 5 degrees.

Basic Movement
1½'
rod lift, immediate return

Side View   Use mostly a wrist movement   Top View

More Aggressive Movement
3'
Use more lower-arm movement.
Top View   Side View
pump   return

2'
Three consecutive rod pumps.
Top View
return
pump   pump
Side View   pump   pump   pump

The KastMaster And Swedish Pimple

Kastmaster

Tie direct to split ring or snap.

Make sure the hook swings easily on the split ring.

Add a single hook at least one-size larger than the original treble to fish a live minnow hooked through the lips or under the dorsal fin.

Swedish Pimple

Basic Movement
1½'
rod lift, immediate return

Use a wrist and lower-arm movement.

Lure flutters as it falls.

More Aggressive Movement
2'

More aggressive jigging may cause the lure to fall farther to the side.

TROLLING RIPRAP FOR WALLEYES

A nglers sing the praises of man-made rock structure in regions where soft-bottomed reservoirs offer little or no natural walleye spawning habitat. Rock riprap along the faces of dams and causeways creates what Mother Nature forgot to provide: suitable hard-bottomed spawning habitat washed by current, perfect for the deposition and oxygenation of walleye eggs, safe from predators until the fry hatch and scatter into the open-water surface layers of the main lake. This is the ideal spring fish attractor once water temperatures approach the walleye's spawning range of around 45°F.

When

Water temperatures between 42°F and 55°F.

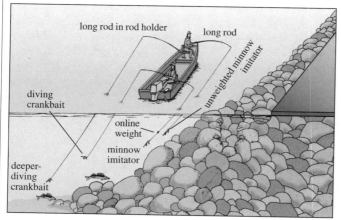

Stagger lures to cover all depths while trolling. Select shallow runners for the inside shallower edge of the dam, diving crankbaits for the deeper outside edge. Pumping hand-held rods usually triggers more fish than trolling with rods in holders.

Tackle

Rods: 7- to 9-foot spinning or casting rods on outside lines and 5½- to 6-foot rods for inside lines. *Reels:* medium-capacity spinning or baitcasting reels. *Line:* 10-pound-test abrasion-resistant monofilament.

Rigging

The key to effective trolling is to stagger lines and lures at different depths to cover the sloping face of the dam or causeway. To best accomplish this, select lures that run at a range of diving depths. Troll the shallowest versions closest to the dam, switching to deeper-running baits farther out. Use different rod lengths to spread lines on the same side of the boat. For example, on the line closest to the dam, longline troll a shallow-running minnow imitator on a 7- to 9-foot rod. Then use a slightly deeper-running lure on the same side of the boat on a 5½- to 6-foot rod. Do the same on the opposite side of the boat, but consider the slope of the rock face and the lure's running depth to reach near or occasionally bounce bottom.

Top Spots On Riprap

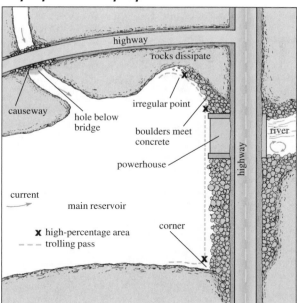

highway

rocks dissipate

irregular point

causeway

hole below bridge

boulders meet concrete

river

powerhouse

highway

current

main reservoir

x high-percentage area

– – – trolling pass

corner

Presentation

When darkness falls, fish move shallow. Use an electric or small outboard motor to move just fast enough to wobble your crankbaits. Proceed parallel along the dam face in a straight path; weaving is unnecessary and usually counterproductive, since it takes baits over open water instead of skimming the face of the rocks. Occasional lure contact with the rocks is fine, but avoid pounding lures—sooner or later you'll snag. Pump hand-held rods occasionally to add a stop-and-go action to lures, making them appear vulnerable or wounded, to further enhance their attractiveness to walleyes. □

DRAGGING JIGS FOR WALLEYES

Though overlooked and seldom used by most of the walleye fishing community, dragging is a popular technique in some parts of the country for presenting jigs, especially in river towns throughout the traditional walleye belt. Keeping a baited leadhead right on the bottom when casting or trolling is more effective than it sounds. And it's also more difficult.

When

Tackle

Rod: 6- to 6½-foot medium-power fast-action spinning rods. *Reel:* medium-capacity spinning reel. *Line:* 8- to 12-pound mono.

Rigging

The weight of the jig depends on the depth of the water fished. Most anglers believe a heavy jig is better for dragging, but a lighter jig usually provides a more natural presentation. Use the lightest jig that will maintain bottom contact, and change jigs as you move to different depths or vary retrieve speeds.

Presentation

Moving a jig while maintaining bottom contact seems relatively simple. It's ultra-slow with light heads and just slow with heavy heads. The key to the technique's

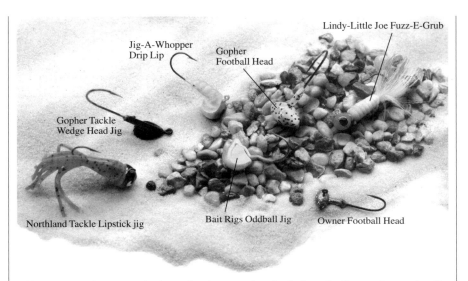

Lindy-Little Joe Fuzz-E-Grub

Jig-A-Whopper
Drip Lip

Gopher
Football Head

Gopher Tackle
Wedge Head Jig

Northland Tackle Lipstick jig

Bait Rigs Oddball Jig

Owner Football Head

effectiveness, however, is the action imparted to the bait as the jig catches and pulls against bottom features.

The action that triggers best is a tail-up activity. The jig has to roll forward on its head, not sideways. With the jighead still anchored to the bottom, the hook and the minnow must rock straight up, as if ready to do a somersault. Walleyes most often strike when the face of the jig digs in and grabs, and the butt pivots up.

Anchored and casting, drifting in the wind or current, or backtrolling all provide potential opportunities to drag. When drifting or trolling, get the jig back. From an anchored position, though, walleyes often hit right at the point where the line becomes vertical. Just as the jig is lifted from the bottom, they hit.

Whether you're casting, drifting, or trolling, keep the rod tip low and close to the water for better feel. When casting, just pull the rod tip parallel to the surface of the water. At times, a long pause—sometimes a long, long pause—triggers more strikes. With the rod tip low, maintaining bottom contact and setting hooks is easier. □

Hooking Position

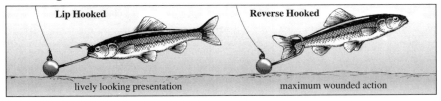

Lip Hooked

Reverse Hooked

lively looking presentation

maximum wounded action

Reversing a minnow—tipping a minnow to a jig by hooking it through the base of the tail instead of the lips—produces a more distressed action that often triggers more strikes.

SLIPPING CURRENT FOR RIVER WALLEYES

Slipping is the term river fishermen use to describe the slow, careful process of using river current to move a boat slowly downstream, carefully controlling boat speed and direction. Simultaneously, as you control the motion of the boat, the moving boat controls the motion of your line and lure. One follows the other, orchestrated by how efficiently you master the process.

When

Presentation

Point your outboard or electric motor directly into the current and exert just enough throttle to hold the boat in place. Now drop your jig or other lure to the bottom, and let out enough line to make contact when you lift-drop the lure. Once you determine the proper combination, back off lightly on the throttle. The boat will begin to drift slowly downstream. The more you reduce throttle, the faster the boat and lure move.

Assuming you've selected the proper jig weight for the current conditions—probably 1/4- or 3/8-ounce—the jig should move slightly ahead of the boat. Tap it along ahead of you, feeling for changes in bottom and for biting fish before the boat ever reaches them. This is a perfect combination for moving slowly downstream in modest current. In faster current, more throttle, a heavier jig, and a longer line are needed.

34

Basic Slipping

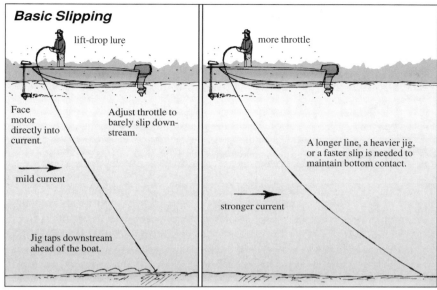

lift-drop lure

Face motor directly into current.

Adjust throttle to barely slip downstream.

mild current

Jig taps downstream ahead of the boat.

more throttle

A longer line, a heavier jig, or a faster slip is needed to maintain bottom contact.

stronger current

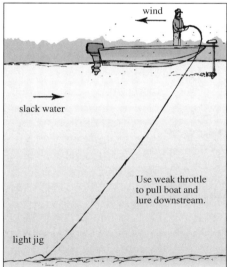

wind

slack water

Use weak throttle to pull boat and lure downstream.

light jig

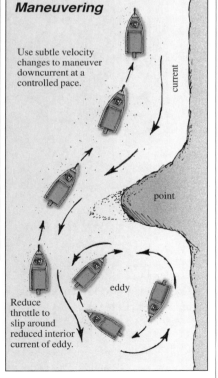

Maneuvering

Use subtle velocity changes to maneuver downcurrent at a controlled pace.

current

point

eddy

Reduce throttle to slip around reduced interior current of eddy.

Use a subtle turn of your motor to change the direction of your downstream movement, from a drift to a directional maneuver. Steer the boat toward a visible edge until the lure and line intersect the change. Immediately turn your motor back slightly in the opposite direction to stop boat movement to the side. Now slowly drift your jig downstream, right along the current edge, making slight adjustments in direction to follow the surface edge. □

SPLIT-SHOT RIGS FOR WALLEYES IN SHALLOW WATER

In shallow water, split-shot rigs are as versatile as jigs. And throughout the season, they often outproduce jigs, especially during tough bites. And in clear water with little wind, when the fish are shallow but difficult to approach, split-shot rigs consistently outproduce everything else. In fact, split-shot rigs should be your first choice whenever conditions include clear water, bright sun, and a calm surface.

When

Tackle

Rod: 6½- to 7½-foot medium-light-power spinning rod. **Reel:** small-capacity spinning reel. **Line:** 4- to 8-pound-test limp mono.

Rigging

Balance tackle to conditions. Heavy wind and short lines require a heavier shot, maybe 1/8 ounce or more, placed 12 to 18 inches up the line. Calm conditions call for long lines, up to 100 feet or so behind the boat, with a single BB placed 4 feet up the line. Experiment with different weights, based on wind and depth, in order to keep the bait swimming slowly just above the bottom.

In spring, carry minnows, leeches, and crawlers. The first four walleyes might come on minnows, the next two on leeches, and the next on a crawler. Some days, all the fish come on one bait, or you might notice a preference change as the day wears on, so cover all the bases. Run crawlers nose-first onto long Aberdeen hook, or onto a two-hook harness. Hook leeches through the sucker, minnows through the lips.

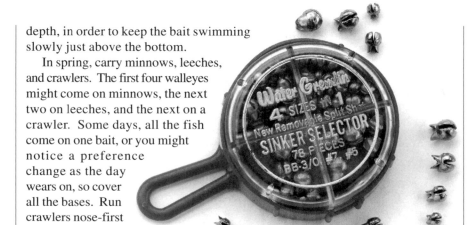

Presentation

No matter the conditions, walleyes in shallow water always are spookier than deeper fish. Have at least 50 feet of line out, but beyond 100 feet or so, rig control is lost. Feeling out the conditions to create that proper blend of weight, distance, line diameter, and leader length is a daily process.

Mustad Finesse

VMC Vanadium

Daiichi baitholder

Gamakatsu glow octopus

Eagle Claw Featherlite

Split-shot rigs troll nicely, but, depending on where fish are located, drifting might be better, positioning the boat sideways with a drift sock to cover a wider swath. In heavy wind, try backtrolling. In a light breeze, try trolling with a bowmount trolling motor. In developing weeds, pitching is an option.

Split-shot rigs must be fished slower than a jig. A minnow tends to move more freely, and leeches or crawlers have time to work at a slower pace. Fish it slow, but not necessarily on bottom. With lighter shot, swim rigs slowly off bottom over developing weeds or wood cover. And give livebait time to trigger bites. ☐

SPAWN-TIME BLUEGILLS

As water temperatures push toward 65°F, bluegills move toward potential spawning areas. Groups of bluegills scatter across flats, usually holding near weed cover. Under stable weather and rising water temperature, they may also roam shallow, searching for areas of favored bottom type, ranging from fine sand mixed with silt to coarse gravel. These bedding colonies provide easy fishing. And because it's adults-only, large fish are more concentrated than at any other time of year.

When

Tackle

Rod: 6- to 12-foot light-power spinning rod or 10- to 20-foot pole. *Reel:* lightweight spinning reel. *Line:* 4- or 6-pound-test limp mono.

Rigging

Bait choice isn't critical. Crickets and red worms are popular throughout the South, while maggots and leeches are often used in the North. Big bluegills also like tiny jigs, plain or tipped with a maggot or piece of night crawler. Suspend baits beneath a sensitive float to detect subtle strikes.

Location

Monitor water temperature to determine when to begin searching for spawning fish. Search sheltered coves, creek arms, or channels where temperatures are higher than in the main body of water. In rivers, look for sloughs or oxbows with slack current—current on the nest can smother the eggs with silt, so bluegills avoid it.

Bluegills generally nest close to shore, in depths that allow nests to be seen from a boat or shore. In areas that appear to offer appropriate water temperature, shelter, and bottom type, look for pale circles 8 to 12 inches in

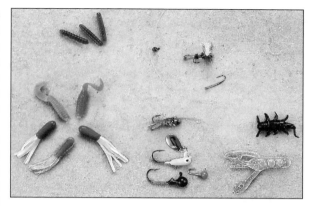

Livebait and flies are fine options for bedding bluegills. But when fish are aggressive, nothing beats small leadhead jigs with tube or twistertail bodies. A drop of glue keeps plastic bodies from sliding off the jig, while floats and casting bubbles increase casting distance and bite detection.

diameter. Anchoring allows the quickest and most efficient fishing from a boat. Wading is also productive.

Presentation

Male bluegills rarely feed during the spawn, but instinctively strike livebaits and small jigs presented near nests. Fish slightly deeper near bedding colonies for pre-spawn females and males between nesting efforts. If you spook fish from a spawning area, back off and they'll return. If you're one of the first anglers to fish a spawning colony, it's often easy to catch 5 or 10 fish before they become wary. □

Bluegill Spawning Locations

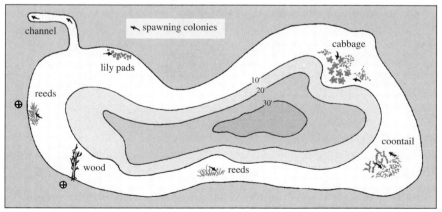

The population of spawning bluegills in ponds, lakes, and reservoirs is often so large that the fish don't all fit into one or two spots. Look for shallow areas that provide a suitable bottom and protective cover.

SUMMER PATTERNS FOR BIG BLUEGILLS

The hunt for trophy predatory fish like bass, walleye, and pike is a process. Good fishermen start with the most likely pattern, given the time of year, then move on to the next, systematically eliminating unproductive water and techniques. Many bluegill fishermen, on the other hand, are stuck in a rut. They anchor on the same weedbed they've been fishing for years and haul out the worms and bobbers. But big bluegills are more likely roaming open water than mingling with peanut panfish in the weeds. And catching them requires a different approach.

When

Tackle

Rod: 5- to 7-foot light-power spinning rod. *Reel:* lightweight spinning reel with long-cast spool. *Line:* 2- to 6-pound-test limp mono.

Common Summer Bluegill Patterns

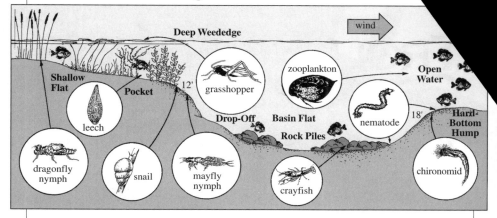

Presentation

Large lakes with lots of deep open-water areas often grow the biggest bluegills. On a typical summer day, consider 6 basic patterns.

Pockets on Flats—Look for weed flats with gravel or rocky areas forming pockets with multiple edges. Pockets also form where low weeds meet high weeds, where pads meet reeds or coontail, and around weed clumps. These areas suggest variations in bottom content and multiple food sources like nymphs, snails, and leeches.

Deep Weededges—Look for the outside or deep edge of the weedline. Predators prowl here, so only the biggest bluegills stay. Wind-driven plankton are corralled by the weed wall. Multiple forage types make these edges good all year.

Deep-Lying Rocks—Look for rocky drop-offs. Check shallow on rock slides as well as the deep-lying base of a slide. Or look for rock piles on flats 15 to 40 feet deep. These bulls feed on small crustaceans, nematodes, nymphs, and other organisms.

Hard-Bottom Humps—Look for submerged islands and humps with gravel or marl. Big bluegills find crawling and burrowing nymphs or aquatic worms in mud, sand, or marl on top of those elements.

Open Water—Wind shifting away from a weedline moves plankton over open water. Big gills follow if plankton are plentiful. Bluegills stay above the thermocline, typically concentrating 10 to 18 feet down.

Terrestrials—Look for insects like grasshoppers blown onto the lake. Bulls from the flats and weedline move shallow in the evening or during the day when offshore winds are strongest. Bluegills feeding on plankton may switch to this pattern if zooplankton decline in late summer. □

41

ꟿLLING FOR CRAPPIES

When warming trends heat the back ends of shallow coves and creek arms in spring, crappies in lakes and reservoirs begin filtering into shallow cover to feed, then to spawn. For most crappie fishermen, the early season begins with that first startling visage of calico slabs hovering in the embrace of wood near shore.

But some crappie fishermen have learned how to jump the gun on this traditional opener. Discovering that crappies stage and suspend in open water adjacent to early spring feeding sites, these anglers troll a spread of diving minnowbaits on flatlines and planer boards.

When

Tackle

Rod: 6- to 7-foot medium-light-power spinning rod. *Reel:* small-capacity spinning reel. *Line:* 4- or 6-pound-test mono.

Rigging

Running a spread of four lines—a planer board line on each side of the boat and two flatlines straight out the back—allows you to cover water quickly and efficiently as you search for active fish. Small crankbaits and minnowbaits are effective, but rigging these baits

Three-Way Trolling Rig

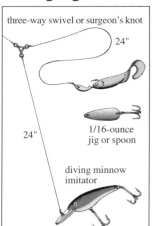

three-way swivel or surgeon's knot

24"

24"

1/16-ounce jig or spoon

diving minnow imitator

in tandem with jigs and spoons often triggers more fish. Tie a three-way swivel to your main line and attach two 24-inch leaders to the remaining swivel loops. To one leader, attach a diving lure designed to reach a depth just above the level where fish are holding. Tie a 1/16-ounce jig or small spoon to the other leader.

Location

In hill-land reservoirs, crappies migrate up creek arms to suspend and stage. Classic location is in the back one-third of the arm. Specific areas are determined by a variety of comfort factors, including depth, forage, water clarity, and temperature. In lakes, crappies move into shallow bays, coves, and boat channels to feed in early spring. During warm, stable weather, they relate to shallow shoreline cover. Cold fronts move them back outside shallow bays or to the center of deeper bays with at least a 25-foot maximum depth. Locating suspended crappies is the same in either environment—move slowly through bays or creek arms as you watch the depthfinder. □

Suspension Zone In A Hill-Land Reservoir

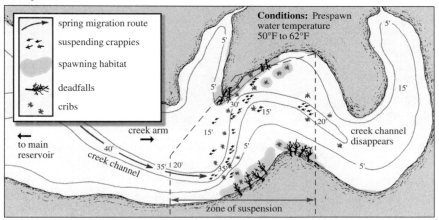

Suspension Zones In Lakes

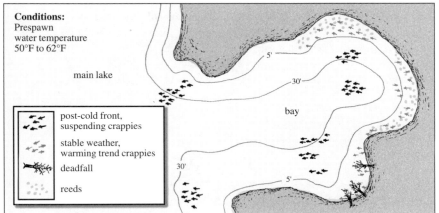

PROBING WEEDLINES FOR YELLOW PERCH

The weedline is an interface between two worlds. Blue expanses, deep structure, and basin flats are present on one side of this green dimension, while shallow, fertile flats extend to shore on the other. In most lakes, most perch opt for deep water. But some use weed flats and weededges all summer, then move deep as winter approaches, following the warmest water, which is present in basins after turnover. Even though shallow fish tend to scatter along weededges, this pattern remains one of the easiest ways to locate catchable numbers. In many places, a daily limit of perch is 25, and that many can easily be caught on weededges in an afternoon.

When

Tackle

Rod: 6- to 7-foot light-power spinning rod. *Reel:* medium-capacity spinning reel. *Line:* 2- or 4-pound-test mono.

Working A Weedline

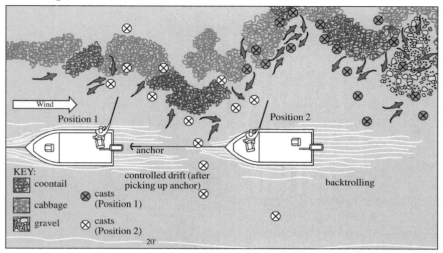

KEY:
- coontail
- cabbage
- gravel
- ⊗ casts (Position 1)
- ⊗ casts (Position 2)
- ⊗ controlled drift (after picking up anchor)
- ⊗ backtrolling

20'

Rigging

Keep your lure options simple. Casting a 1/32-ounce jig tipped with a crayfish tail or piece of crawler, or a small spinner rig baited with a small leech or red worm will catch most of the perch you encounter.

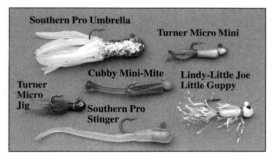

Southern Pro Umbrella
Turner Micro Mini
Cubby Mini-Mite
Lindy-Little Joe Little Guppy
Turner Micro Jig
Southern Pro Stinger

Location

Throughout the day, perch often maintain positions just inside the weededge or right at the base of the weeds. They also may bunch up in specific spots on the adjacent flat, but these fish are harder to locate and keep up with. Look for irregularities in the weedline. A gravel or rock finger extending from an open pocket in the weeds, an inside turn at the base of a point in the weedline, or a change in density or type of weedgrowth attracts more perch and holds them longer.

Presentation

First casts determine the layout of the weededge. Next, cast over the weeds. Swim the jig over the weed tops and drop it down the edge. Crappies might hold on top of the weeds, but perch usually strike as the jig drops to the base of the weeds. Then cast parallel to the edge and let the jig fall all the way to the bottom before lift-dropping it back along the edge. Move the boat to the edge of your previous casting range and repeat the presentation sequence. □

CLASSIC RIGS FOR PANFISH

Rigs are a time-honored tra-
dition among panfishermen,
the oldest and most recognizable
being the crappie spreader. In
most instances, rigs cover water
quicker than bobber dunking,
fly-fishing, or pitching jigs.
Rigs also can be designed for
specific tasks, such as covering
a variety of depths at once with
multiple jig setups, or pulling
big crappies out of heavy timber
with welding-rod rigs. Unlike
jigs and flies, though, which
offer precise control of bait
position, fish sometimes bite
rigs without being felt.
Knowing when to rig and when
to pitch or fly-cast is the key to
consistent panfishing.

When

Shallow Water Rigging

The best way to hunt for spawning crappies and bluegills is with a split-shot rig or
simple sliding sinker rig. Use single hooks baited with small leeches or crickets for
bluegills, small minnows for crappies. Worms require tandem-hook rigs, but leeches
and minnows work better most days. Pitch the rig into likely spawning cover as you
drift along a drop-off, then anchor and cast when you locate a concentration of fish.

Deep Water Rigging

Tie a tandem-hook rig on a leader, slide four small beads down to the hooks, and
slide on a clevis connected to a #00 or up to a #1 Indiana spinner blade. Tie on the
swivel to complete a versatile rig. The blade adds flash and thump for attraction.
How much flash and thump depends on size. Size #00 and #0 blades don't spin
much. On 4-pound-test rigs, a #1 blade spins and thumps much better. Make your
selection based on water clarity and the aggressiveness of the fish.

A spinner rig can be adapted for use with minnows, red worms, crawlers, or leeches. Used alone or with a single spilt shot, the rig drifts or trolls efficiently from depths of one foot down to 10 feet—perfect for high-riding suspended crappies and bluegills. It also can be presented behind small bottom bouncers or three-way rigs. Or it can be fished on a long line directly behind the boat. It's even possible to pitch and retrieve it over weeds in shallower water.

Open Water Rigging

One of the best options for suspended crappies, white bass, and bluegills is to drift with multiple jig rigs. By fishing with two or more jigs on one line, one rod can cover two or more depths at the same time. Multiple rods can cover the entire water column at two-foot intervals. Tie two loops into the main line at two- or three-foot intervals from the end, for attaching 6-inch loop end leaders. The end of the line can hold a larger jig or a bell sinker, with lighter jigs on the leaders. □

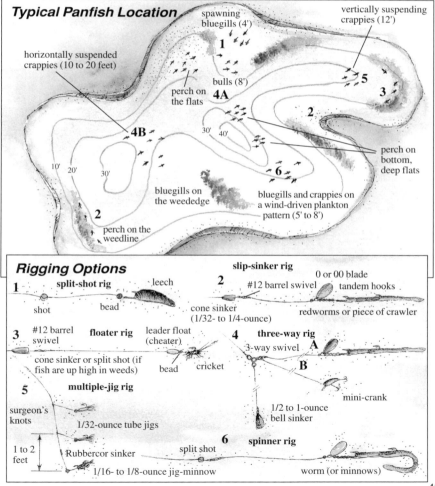

Typical Panfish Location

spawning bluegills (4')

vertically suspending crappies (12')

horizontally suspended crappies (10 to 20 feet)

bulls (8')

perch on the flats **4A**

1

5

3

2

4B   30'   40'

perch on bottom, deep flats

10'   20'   30'

6

2

bluegills on the weededge

bluegills and crappies on a wind-driven plankton pattern (5' to 8')

perch on the weedline

Rigging Options

1 **split-shot rig**   leech

shot   bead

2 **slip-sinker rig**   0 or 00 blade
#12 barrel swivel   tandem hooks

cone sinker (1/32- to 1/4-ounce)   redworms or piece of crawler

3 #12 barrel swivel **floater rig** leader float (cheater)

cone sinker or split shot (if fish are up high in weeds)   bead   cricket

4 **three-way rig**
3-way swivel **A**

B

mini-crank

5 **multiple-jig rig**

surgeon's knots

1/32-ounce tube jigs

1/2 to 1-ounce bell sinker

1 to 2 feet

Rubbercor sinker   split shot

6 **spinner rig**

1/16- to 1/8-ounce jig-minnow   worm (or minnows)

BLUE CATFISH FROM COLD WATER

Veteran catmen know that blue cats, more than channels or flatheads, are creatures of big rivers and impoundments. They know, too, that big blues like more current than either of their whiskered cousins. Until recently, however, few people were aware of the blue cat's love of cold water.

Instead of sticking their belly to the bottom of a hole for the winter, these fish continue to forage in chutes of swift current when water temperatures drop to 35°F. In river-run reservoirs across much of the blue cat's range, the period from December through March may be the best time to tangle with a monster blue.

When

Tackle

Rod: 6- to 8-foot medium-heavy-power casting rod. *Reel:* large-capacity casting reel with a freespool clicker. *Line:* 20- to 40-pound-test abrasion-resistant mono.

Rigging

A basic slip rig consisting of a 1- to 6-ounce egg sinker sliding on the main line, which is tied to a 1- to 3-foot leader consisting of a hook, line, and swivel. Several 1-inch cubes of cutbait packed neatly on a 7/0 Kahle-style hook don't roll as much in current as a long strip of bait.

Location

During winter and early spring, big blue cats run the river channel, feeding along channel ledges. They rarely move onto adjacent shallow flats. Even hot-water discharges don't attract big blue cats, although they do draw one of the blue cat's favorite baitfish, the skipjack herring. A discharge area is a prime spot to gather fresh herring for cutbait.

Area A—The head of a narrow river section before the river widens and flattens is a prime area for blue cats that hesitate to move farther upriver into decreasing current. Use sonar to run upriver along the channel ledge, looking for nooks and debris that attract and hold fish. A particularly good area is where the ledge begins to push away from the bank to form a large shallow flat.

Area B—The entire ledge is a potential holding area for blue cats. Try the ledge area near the final barge tie-off. Should be a big eddy here, too. Note also how the ledge pushes away from the bank near the beginning of the discharge area—good spot. The head of a deep channel area as it pushes into a shallower area is another hot spot for big blues.

Area C—First check the ledge area where the shallow flat extends into the channel below the discharge inlet. Then note how the flat cuts back toward the bluff bank, creating another possible holding area. Be sure to run along the ledge near the bluff bank—limestone outcroppings are particularly craggy and difficult to fish, but often hold big blues. ☐

Typical Flowing Reservoir

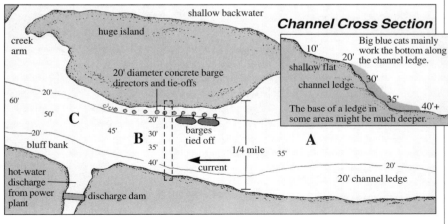

49

CATFISH LOCATION IN SMALL RIVERS

The easiest way to understand catfish location in rivers is to look at small streams. Small streams are easier to get to know because the catfish's world is compressed into a small area. In a large river, major holes may be half a mile apart. On a small stream, however, half a mile might contain 10 holes. You can move and see lots of water. More importantly, the continuing combination of riffles, holes, and runs, and the cover elements that may exist in them are obvious. Small rivers offer the quickest education in river anatomy and how catfish relate to it.

When

Riffle-Hole-Run

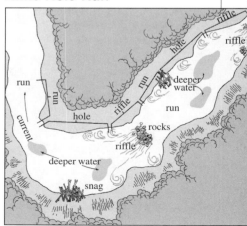

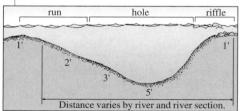

Rivers consist of a continuous series of riffles, holes, and runs.

Tackle

Rod: 7- to 12-foot casting or spinning rod. *Reel:* medium-capacity baitcasting or spinning reel. *Line:* 10- to 20-pound-test abrasion-resistant mono.

Location

Riffles form when a river washes over a hard bottom. A pool of water builds at the head of a riffle, eventually overflowing and pushing over the constricted area like water forced through the nozzle of a hose. The force of current flowing against the softer substrate at the end of a riffle scours a hole. Holes are the home of catfish. The depth of a hole varies according to current velocity and the size of the river, but all holes are deeper and wider than riffle and run areas in the same section of stream. Holes gradually become shallower at their downstream end as current slows and suspended materials settle to the river bottom. The tail end of a hole becomes a run—a river flat.

Catfish often move upstream to smaller water during spring and early summer, then back downstream into bigger water during late summer and early fall. During winter, catfish must gather in holes with sufficient depth, current, and oxygen to sustain them throughout the cold-water period. Such holes are most likely in downriver sections. Flatheads rarely move more than one tributary away from a major river, while channel cats may move into tiny creeks several tributaries removed from a major river. Blue cats, even more than flatheads, are fish of big rivers. Smaller blues may push upriver into the beginning stretches of tributary streams, but the biggest blues usually stay in big water. ☐

Holding Areas In A Typical Hole

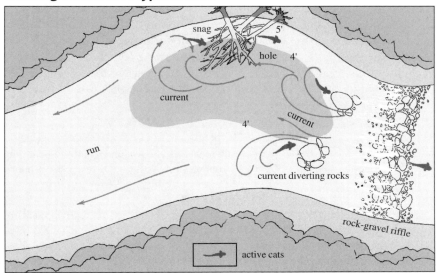

Inactive cats usually hold in the snag or in deeper water in a hole. Active cats feed near the snag but just as likely leave the snag and (1) move ahead of the riffle to feed in the fast slick water; (2) find a spot to hold in and wait for food below the riffle; or (3) roam the hole, searching for food.

TROLLING CRANKBAITS FOR CATFISH

No surprise, given how sound sensitive and vibration sensitive catfish are, that they crunch their share of crankbaits all across the country—crankbaits of various styles in lakes, rivers, and reservoirs, mainly during summer and into fall, but also throughout late spring on some waters. Most of these catches are accidental, but fishing crankbaits for cats make sense. When it comes to processing messages from their environment, catfish are one of the most sensitive of all freshwater fish. Their sense of hearing, which works in combination with their lateral line sense to detect the sounds and vibrations emitted by their prey, is more sensitive than those of bass, pike, and other species commonly pursued with artificial lures.

When

Tackle

Rod: 7½-foot flippin' stick. **Reel:** medium-capacity baitcasting reel. **Line:** 28-pound fused filament line and a 10-foot section of 20-pound-test mono leader.

Rigging

Most river trollers rely on shallow-running banana baits or minnowbaits tied on a three-way or Carolina rig weighted with a 1- or 2-ounce sinker to reach the depths where active cats often hold in rivers. Deep-running crankbaits like the Manns 20+ and Storm Lightnin' Shad, though, can be trolled to depths of 20 or more feet without weights. Cats typically aren't boat shy, so line length should be determined by depth and current velocity. Continue to pay out line until the plug occasionally ticks bottom as the boat moves slowly upstream.

Location

Catfish in rivers often concentrate in deep holes during the day, particularly holes at bends in the main river channel. Depending on the size and depth of the hole and the amount of cover present, deep-running or weighted crankbaits can sometimes be trolled near bottom through the core of the hole. If the hole is too deep or the bottom too snaggy, troll baits near the drop-off around the perimeter of the hole or over shallow flats adjacent to deeper water where active cats often forage after dark.

Presentation

Moving upstream creates more water resistance on the lip of a crankbait, causing baits to dive deeper and swim with more action. Instead of placing your rod in a rod holder, though, sweep the rod tip

Catfish Trolling Rigs

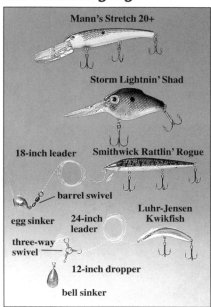

Mann's Stretch 20+

Storm Lightnin' Shad

18-inch leader   Smithwick Rattlin' Rogue

barrel swivel

egg sinker   24-inch leader   Luhr-Jensen Kwikfish

three-way swivel

12-inch dropper

bell sinker

forward a foot or two every 10 seconds or so, which causes the bait to wiggle enticingly to trigger fish in a neutral feeding mood. Keep a close eye on sonar, too. Blue cats and sometimes flatheads and channel cats may suspend several feet off the bottom to feed on shad and other baitfish. If you see a big fish or a school of bait on your display, move your bait to the same depth. ☐

Trolling Crankbaits In Smaller Rivers

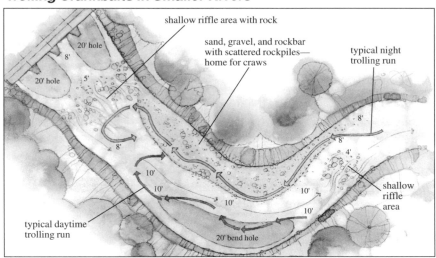

shallow riffle area with rock

20' hole

8'

20' hole   5'

sand, gravel, and rockbar with scattered rockpiles— home for craws

typical night trolling run

8'

8'

4'

10'

10'

10'

10'

10'

10'

shallow riffle area

typical daytime trolling run

20' bend hole

53

NATURAL BAITS FOR CATFISH

Scientific studies show that catfish can detect several amino acids—the substances that comprise all food—at concentrations of just one part per 100 million. They can taste the difference between a creek chub and a baby carp at 50 paces. In rivers, current constantly carries attractive and displeasing scents and tastes to cats. In still water, cats tend to move more, sampling the water for potential food. They disregard most sensations, just as our ears, eyes, and noses tune out most incoming stimuli. What grabs their interest are the scents and flavors emitted by familiar prey.

When

Livebait

When choosing natural baits, one constant question is whether to use a whole live baitfish or cut sections. Flatheads, particularly big ones, usually prefer active livebaits that live for hours on the hook and actively try to escape. Flatheads can be caught on deadbait and cutbait, of course, particularly when they're first emerging from their wintering holes and when their activity level peaks prior to spawning in early to midsummer. Throughout the rest of the season, though, targeting big flatheads with anything other than a large lively baitfish is a low-percentage call.

Cutbait

Channel, blue, and white cats, though, usually prefer baits that are easy to catch over those that are lively. Cutting a fish frees proteins and amino acids in the flesh, along with blood, a sure attractant. These molecules drift in the water where they are detected by the smell and taste organs of nearby catfish. Cats, sensing something edible, approach the source, then use taste buds located on their barbels, mouth, and skin to make a final assessment of the bait. Catfish accustomed to eating a particular prey species quickly detect its scent and taste, readily accepting it as food.

Rigging

Consider how the bait can best be presented to the fish, then choose the simplest, cleanest rig to deliver and hold the bait in the right location. The least number of components in the rig means fewer components to fail and knots to break, and less weight to interfere with a natural presentation. The versatile sliprig is a good choice for most situations in lakes, rivers, and reservoirs. Three-way rigs are better suited to drifting in lakes and reservoirs, or still fishing in heavy current. Run the hook point through a corner of a piece of cutbait, or through the lips or tail muscle of a whole baitfish. In either case, leave the hook point exposed. □

Sliprig

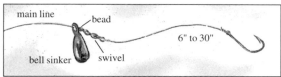

main line
bead
6" to 30"
bell sinker
swivel

Three-Way Rig

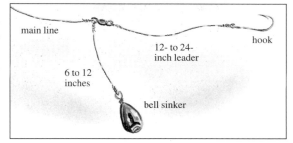

main line
hook
12- to 24-
inch leader
6 to 12
inches
bell sinker

55

FINDING & CATCHING CHANNEL CATFISH IN PONDS

A cross the country, more fishing opportunities for catfish exist in ponds than in any other kind of water. Within the "pond belt" region from northern Virginia to southern Montana, more than 1,000 new ponds are built each year. And unless large natural lakes predominate in your area, several ponds usually can be found within a 10-mile radius of your home. To consistently catch channel cats in the 10-pound class, locate and gain access to the most productive ponds in your area.

When

Tackle

Rod: 6½- to 7½-foot medium-power spinning or casting rod. *Reel:* medium-capacity spinning or casting reel. *Line:* 10- to 14-pound-test mono.

Rigging

Slipsinker rigs baited with nightcrawlers, cutbait, sour bait, or crayfish tails is the most common approach. Slipfloats rigs remain an overlooked option in most parts of the country, but they may present baits more efficiently that set rigs. Slipfloats allow you to instantly change the level at which a bait is suspended, by sliding a stop knot up or down the line. Use a float to hold baits near the surface for channel cats suspended over deep water, or as a strike indicator when baits are fished on the bottom for cats cruising in shallower water.

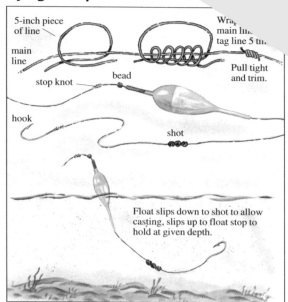

Tying A Stop Knot

5-inch piece of line

main line

Wrap main line, tag line 5 tn.

Pull tight and trim.

stop knot — bead

hook

shot

Float slips down to shot to allow casting, slips up to float stop to hold at given depth.

Location

In ponds, as in rivers, holes often key catfish location. Catfish winter in the deepest holes of the pond and prowl adjacent structure like points, cuts, and flats during the open-water season. In ponds without feeder creeks or other sources of oxygen, the pond may stratify during late summer. With the depths devoid of oxygen, small channel cats often roam the shallows, but the biggest fish usually suspend over deep water. Current areas created by creeks, springs, or pumps also are worth checking.

Presentation

In private ponds with little fishing pressure and a strong catfish population, a few cats usually can be caught at any time of the day on almost any kind of bait. But the biggest cats in ponds, especially in ponds with moderate fishing pressure, often are difficult to catch. Fishing at night with natural baits usually is more effective than fishing during the day. Chumming a small area of the pond with fermented grain, a commercial chum mixture, or dry dog food attracts and holds active channel cats that otherwise would roam along weededges and drop-offs. □

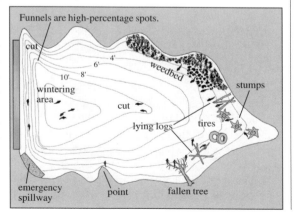

Built Pond

Funnels are high-percentage spots.

cut

6' 4'

10' 8'

weedbed

wintering area

cut

stumps

lying logs

tires

emergency spillway

point

fallen tree

RIGS FOR PIKE

Successful guides, those with fashionably clothed wives and well-fed children, often have a bait or two reserved for the toughest conditions—a lure that produces fish and income during the doggiest days of summer. The Lindy Spin Rig was such a weapon. The simplicity and productivity of the rig almost guaranteed pike for skilled and unskilled clients alike. Just hook a big minnow through the lips, cast it out, and catch pike all afternoon. While the Spin Rig is no longer made, the Gopher Bait Spin, a variety of skirtless short-arm spinnerbait, or a homemade rig of similar design still produces pike.

When

Tackle

Rod: 6½- to 7½-foot medium-heavy-power casting or spinning rod. *Reel:* medium-capacity baitcasting or spinning reel. *Line:* 12- or 14-pound-test mono.

Rigging

It's not unusual to tie directly to a spin rig with monofilament and to fish for several days without getting bitten off, then suddenly be cut off by the next half dozen fish. Depends on the size of the fish and how they strike the bait. The problem with these lures is the open line-tie loop. The snap at the terminal end of a commercial wire leader often slides up the arm of the bait.

Make your own leaders from 18- or 27-pound-test noncoated stranded wire. Cut a piece about 14 inches long. Wrap the wire twice through a small swivel, leaving

Use lively minnows ranging from 3½ to 5½ inches. Shiners and creek chubs are favored, but suckers and other minnows also work well. For casting or trolling, insert the hook into the minnow's mouth and out through the middle of the head.

a 1-inch tag. Lock a forceps on the end of the tag. Now, while holding the swivel with one hand and the leader with the other, swing the forceps forward around the leader. Repeat the process to secure the bait to the wire.

Presentation

A combination casting and trolling approach allows anglers to cover more water and trigger more active fish than either method individually. The boat driver trolls a 3/8-ounce Spin Rig and medium chub or shiner while watching the depthfinder to maintain contact with a drop-off on the edge of a weed flat. One or two additional anglers can cast 3/8- or 1/2-ounce Spin Rigs up onto the flat, retrieving the lures over and through weed clumps. When the lure loses contact with the weeds, pause to let the bait flutter down on a tight line. □

Combo Casting And Backtrolling

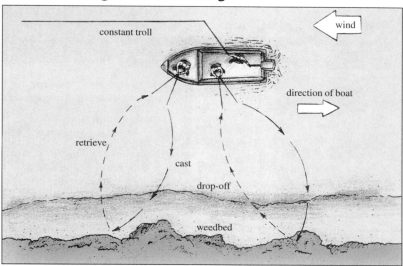

A combination approach usually used along the drop-off on a weed flat will work along any edge. You might also troll forward using a bowmount electric motor. The angler trolling should intermittently "pump" the spin rig forward, then let is slowly drift back, a prime triggering maneuver.

SPEED TROLLING FOR PIKE

O nce summer sets in, the outside weedline is the focal point for pike activity in most natural lakes and reservoirs. In clear lakes, the deep edge of the weedline may run 12 to 17 or even 20 feet deep, the average being 10 to 15 feet. And in murky lakes, it may be as shallow

as 4 to 7 feet. Points and inside turns in the outside weededge on major main-lake bars usually attract pike, mainly because these areas are passing or gathering points for baitfish— perch, bullheads, ciscoes, suckers, or small gamefish, depending on the body of water.

When

Tackle

Rod: 7½-foot flippin' stick for smaller baits and a 6- to 7-foot muskie bucktail rod for larger baits. **Reel:** widespool baitcasting reel. **Line:** 14- to 17-pound-test abrasion-resistant mono or 20-pound-test monel wire line.

Rigging

If you don't use wire line, you need a wire leader. Buy leaders with a Cross-Lok snap on the terminal end and a good swivel on the other end, or make your own from 27-pound-test single-strand wire.

Presentation

Run crankbaits behind a boat moving forward at 3 to 7 mph just outside the edge of the weeds. With two fishermen each using one rod, run one lure about mid-depth, the other a foot or two off the bottom. Pike have an ultra-sensitive lateral line system that lets them feel baits long before they see them. Different types of plugs give off different vibration patterns. As a rule, tighter patterns caused by a faster vibration work best during early summer. Wider patterns become more productive as summer progresses.

Consider using wire line to get deeper faster and work more efficiently through the edge of weeds. When your lure contacts weeds, rip your rod tip forward to snap the lure through the edge. If weeds hang on the bait, rip several more times to snap them off. The rip also serves as a triggering maneuver. Constantly pump your rod tip forward a foot or two. Then stop and the let the rod tip drift back to its starting position. The lure hustles forward, changing its wobble as it goes, then slows and limps along. Following pike often can't resist the sudden change in action. □

Trolling Weededges

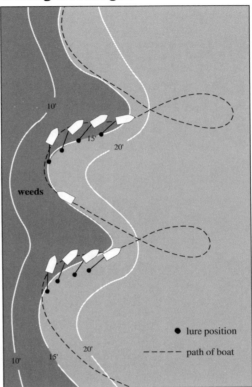

Keep your lines short to follow the weededge as tight as possible. As you approach a turn, let the boat move over the weeds for a short distance, then slowly move back to deeper water. Make an outside turn on points to keep lures on track.

As a rule, begin with small baits (#9 Shad Rap) and use progressively larger baits (#14 Magnum Rapala and #18 Magnum Rapala) as the season progresses.

WEIGHTED BUCKTAILS FOR MUSKIES

Rather than tossing the same bucktails at the same speed as everyone else, consider something muskies haven't seen before. Most bucktails have bushy tails and a large blade, a big cumbersome lure designed to entice a single large fish. But if you want to trigger lots of fish, consider lures at the opposite end of the spectrum—small sparsely tied bucktails with small blades that can be reeled back to the boat at high speed because they're less water-resistant. This not only allows for covering more water, but it adds a high-speed triggering effect that's deadly on muskies in heavily fished waters.

When

Tackle

Rod: 7½-foot flippin' stick or muskie bucktail rod. *Reel:* wide-spool baitcasting reel. *Line:* 20-pound-test abrasion-resistant mono or 27-pound-test dacron.

Bucktail Options

standard large bucktail

standard small bucktail

modified bucktail for long casts and high-speed retrieves

Rigging

Start with a small- to medium-size bucktail like a #5 Blue Fox Musky Buck, Windels Harasser, Fudally Musky Candy, Mepps Musky Killer, or Wahl's Little Eagle Tail. Thin the bucktail dressing by trimming hair at the collar, not the tips. Tips of hair provide all the action, and whole lengths of hair are more attractive and functional than hair stubs. Add 1/2 to 1 ounce of weight by removing the rubber core of a Rubbercor sinker and pinching the sinker around the main shaft or rear hook shank. Add a thin plastic worm tail to the forward hook to give the illusion of bulk without adding water-resistance.

Presentation

Fish weighted bucktails in the same places you fish standard bucktails, but faster. Quickly cover points, bars, humps, reefs, and other muskie hangouts to catch active fish and locate neutral or negative muskies that may be triggered later in the day with a more subtle approach. Long casts and fast retrieves trigger fish that have already seen hundreds of lures. How fast? A bait can't be retrieved fast enough to pull it away from a fish that wants to eat it. Start the retrieve as soon as the lure hits the water, turning the reel handle as fast as possible. If the lure planes too high in the water column, creating a bulging wake on the surface, add more weight to the spinner shaft or use a smaller blade. □

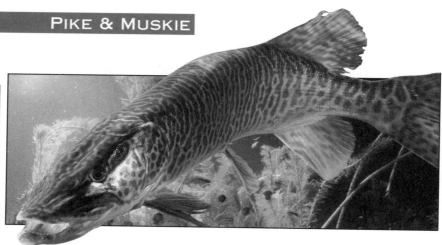

FINDING HYBRID MUSKIES IN NATURAL LAKES

Hybrid muskies—the cross between muskellunge and northern pike—occur in nature where populations of both species coexist. In recent times, fishery departments have recognized the hybrid's value as a gamefish, both in its willingness to bite lures and in its ability to use untapped forage like shad, ciscoes, smelt, and stunted panfish. The key to catching hybrids is understanding their behavior and how it contrasts with the behavior of muskies and pike. During certain conditions, hybrids may be found with either parent species, but in most cases they warrant a unique approach.

When

Tackle

Rod: 7½-foot heavy-power flippin' stick. **Reel:** large-capacity baitcasting reel. **Line:** 20-pound-test abrasion-resistant mono.

Hybrid Location Through The Seasons

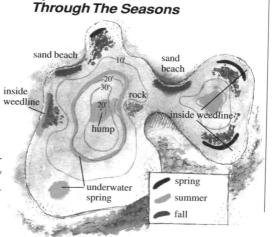

sand beach

sand beach

inside weedline

rock

inside weedline

hump

underwater spring

10'

20'
30'

20'

- spring
- summer
- fall

Rigging

Many traditional muskie lures basically are jumbo versions of popular bass baits. Since hybrid muskies seldom exceed 20 pounds, however, monstrous baits typically aren't necessary to catch them, and may at times be counterproductive. Try anything from popular muskie lures down to larger sizes of comparable bass lures. Most lures designed for pike also are well suited to hybrid muskies.

Location

In spring, back bays and inside weedlines hold numbers of hybrid muskies. In summer, they become more main-lake oriented. While evidence suggests they avoid warm water, at times they move into adjacent shallow areas like rockpiles and inside weededges. If the water doesn't warm too much, they may remain shallow if forage is available. Otherwise, coldwater springs draw fish.

Hybrids also suspend in open water, feeding on crappies or bluegills relating to weededges, but not necessarily tight to the weedline. Humps topping out above the thermocline, the basins of back bays with moderate depth—in other words top crappie spots—become prime holding areas. Following tight to the drop-off and casting atop adjacent weeds or flats may miss fish. Much of the time, hybrids are either deeper or much shallower than most anglers fish.

Cooling water in fall brings hybrids back into shallow water, particularly near the main lake. Both muskies and hybrids lie on shallow sand, soaking up sun this time of year, creating opportunities for sight fishing with lightweight jigs. □

Select Lures For Hybrids

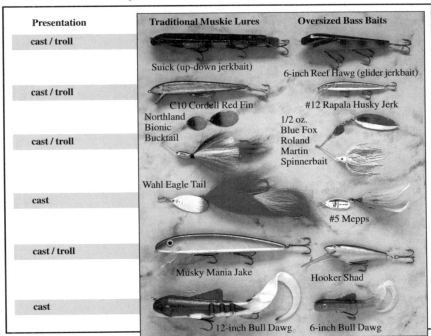

Presentation	Traditional Muskie Lures	Oversized Bass Baits
cast / troll	Suick (up-down jerkbait)	6-inch Reef Hawg (glider jerkbait)
cast / troll	C10 Cordell Red Fin	#12 Rapala Husky Jerk
cast / troll	Northland Bionic Bucktail	1/2 oz. Blue Fox Roland Martin Spinnerbait
cast	Wahl Eagle Tail	#5 Mepps
cast / troll	Musky Mania Jake	Hooker Shad
cast	12-inch Bull Dawg	6-inch Bull Dawg

FINESSE TACTICS FOR PIKE IN SHALLOW WATER

Sometimes—many times—pike are so aggressive early in the season that they chase and inhale nearly anything tossed at them. Other times, even on the best pike waters, pike that have been caught before are wary of chasing certain baits. Some bite, some follow halfheartedly, others barely consider your lure. Yet a subtle presentation right on their noses often, if not most often, does the trick. The key is knowing when and how to adapt.

When

Tackle

Rod: 6½- to 7½-foot medium-power casting or medium-heavy-power spinning rod. *Reel:* medium-capacity baitcasting or spinning reel. *Line:* 14- to 20-pound-test mono with a wire leader.

Soft Plastics

Slug-Go type worm bodies are effective for fishing the surface to 3-foot range and are sufficiently weedless to be fished in and around sparse flooded grass. Near-weightless when rigged with a single hook, an 8-inch Slug-Go ever so slightly sinks before the malevolent yellow eyes watching from below. A twitch

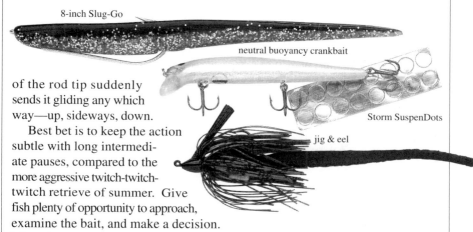

8-inch Slug-Go

neutral buoyancy crankbait

Storm SuspenDots

jig & eel

of the rod tip suddenly sends it gliding any which way—up, sideways, down.

Best bet is to keep the action subtle with long intermediate pauses, compared to the more aggressive twitch-twitch-twitch retrieve of summer. Give fish plenty of opportunity to approach, examine the bait, and make a decision. Many times, you'll see the fish and can react to what it's doing, by pausing or twitching at critical times. The weight of the hook and leader is sufficient to make the bait drift toward bottom like a wounded baitfish.

Minnowbaits

Neutrally buoyant crankbaits like Storm ThunderSticks or Rapala Husky Jerks provide another shallow to mid-depth alternative. These lightly weighted versions of traditional floating minnows dive when pulled, then suspend at rest, hovering before watchful gamefish. Some are slight floaters, others barely sinkers, while perfectly balanced models hang level and vulnerable, neither rising nor sinking.

To fine-tune baits or to make any floater into a neutral-buoyancy bait, add adhesive lead Storm SuspenDots along the belly of the lure, as required. Keep adding and testing until you perfect buoyancy. Balanced baits afford the luxury of being able to stop a lure before a pike's eyes and to let it hang there, even in only a couple of feet of water. Plus, they're slightly heavier than traditional floaters, enabling longer casts.

Jigs

Jigging affords the luxury of being able to target cast to pike at depths of a foot down to 6 or 8 feet, and then keeping the bait almost motionless to trigger them. And plastic tails come in all shapes, sizes, and colors that are easy to carry in resealable plastic bags. The drawback to plastics is that they quickly shred when attacked by toothy critters. Carry a bunch, or run out in a hurry.

Traditional jig and pig bass baits with weedless rubber-skirted jigheads and large pork eel trailers are another option. They offer similar ease of casting and fishability in shallow water, plus have the added attraction of scent. And they come in a range of patterns and sizes, adding bulk to trigger big fish. They're also durable—a handful of jigs and a couple jars of pork can last all season. □

GLOSSARY

Action: Measure of rod performance that describes the bend of a rod; ranges from slow to fast.

Anal Fin: Fin located on the ventral side of most fish, between the anal pore and tail.

Backwater: Shallow area off a river.

Baitfish: Small fish often eaten by predators.

Bar: Long ridge in a body of water. Sometimes called a shoal.

Bay: Major indentation in the shoreline of a lake or reservoir.

Bell Sinker: Pear-shaped sinker with brass eye on top.

Break: Distinct variation in otherwise constant stretches of cover, structure, or bottom type.

Breakline: Area of abrupt change in depth, bottom type, or water quality.

Cabbage: Any of several species of submerged weeds of the genus Potamogeton.

Canal: Man-made waterway for navigation.

Channel: The bed of a stream or river.

Coontail: Submerged aquatic plant of the hornwort family, typically found in hard water; characterized by stiff, forked leaves.

Cove: An indentation along the shoreline of a lake or reservoir.

Cover: Natural or man-made objects on the bottom of lakes, rivers, or impoundments, especially those that influence fish behavior.

Crankbait: Lipped diving lure.

Crustacean: Hard-shelled, typically aquatic invertebrate.

Current: Water moving in one direction, which may be interrupted or redirected over objects.

Dam: Man-made barrier to water flow.

Dark-Bottom Bay: Shallow, protected bay with a layer of dark organic material on the bottom that warms quickly in spring.

Dorsal Fin: Fin located on center of a fish's back.

Drag: System for allowing fish to pull line from reel while antireverse switch is engaged.

Drainage: The area drained by a river and all its tributaries.

Drop-Off: An area of substantial increase in depth.

Eddy: Area of slack water or reversed current in a stream or river.

Egg Sinker: Egg-shaped sinker with a hole from end to end.

Farm Pond: Small man-made body of water.

Feeder Creek: Tributary to a stream.

Feeding Strategy: Behaviors used for capture of prey.

Fingerling: Juvenile fish, usually from 1 to 3 inches long.

Fishing Pressure: Amount of angling on a body of water in a period of time, usually measured in hours per acre per year; its effects on fish populations.

Flat: Area of lake, reservoir, or river characterized by little change in depth; may be shallow or deep.

Flippin': Presentation technique for dropping lures into dense cover at close range.

Flippin' Stick: Heavy-action fishing rod, 7 to 8 feet long, originally designed for bass fishing.

Float: Buoyant device for suspending bait.

Float Stop: Adjustable rubber bead or thread, set on line above float to determine fishing depth.

Fluorescent: Emits radiation when exposed to sunlight.

Forage: Something to be eaten; the act of eating.

Front: Weather system that causes changes in temperature, cloud cover, precipitation, wind, and barometric pressure.

Fry: Recently hatched fish.

Gamefish: Fish species pursued by anglers.

Habitat: Type of environment in which an organism usually lives.

Hole: Deep section of a stream or river.

Hybrid: Offspring of two species or subspecies.

Impoundment: Body of water formed by damming running water (a reservoir).

Invertebrate: Animal without a backbone.

Jig: Lure composed of leadhead with rigid hook, often with hair, plastic, rubber, or other dressings.

Lake: Confined area where water accumulates naturally.

Larva: Immature form of an organism.

Lateral Line: Sensory system of fish that detects low frequency vibrations in water.

Ledge: Sharp contour break in a river or reservoir.

Livebait: Any living animal used to entice fish to bite.

Location: Where fish position themselves in a body of water.

Migration: Directed movement by large number of animals of one species.

Minnowbait: Long, thin, minnow-shaped wood or plastic lure; a wobbling bait.

Monofilament: Fishing line made from a strand of synthetic fiber.

Nymph: Larval form of an insect.

Omnivore: Organism that eats a wide variety of items.

Open Water: The portion of a lake or reservoir away from flats and shoals.

Opportunistic: Feeding strategy in which items are eaten according to availability.

Overharvest: A level of fish harvest from a body of water that substantially reduces abundance of catchable fish, particularly large fish.

Oxbow: A U-shaped bend in a river.

Panfish: Group of about 30 small warmwater sportfish, including bullheads but not catfish.

Pattern: A defined set of location and presentation factors that consistently produce fish.

Pectoral Fin: Paired fin usually located on fish's side behind the head.

Pelagic: Living in open, offshore waters.

Pelvic Fin: Paired fin usually located on lower body.

pH: A measure of hydrogen in concentration.

Phosphorescent: Ability to glow in the dark after exposure to a light source.

Pit: Area excavated for mining operations that fills with water.

Pitching: Presentation technique in which worms or jigs are dropped into cover at close range (15 to 30 feet) with an underhand, pendulum motion, using a 6- to 7-foot casting rod.

Plankton: Organisms drifting in a body of water.

Plug: Solid-bodied wood or plastic lure.

Point: Projection of land into a body of water.

Polarized: Capability of breaking up sunlight into directional components.

Pond: Small natural or manmade body of water.

Pool: Deep section of a stream or river.

Population: Group of animals of the same species within a geographical area that freely interbreed.

Postspawn: Period immediately after spawning; In-Fisherman calendar period between spawn and presummer.

Pound-Test: System for measuring the strength of fishing line; the amount of pressure that will break a line.

Predator: Fish that often feed on other fish.

Presentation: Combination of bait or lure, rig, tackle, and technique used to catch fish.

Prespawn: Period prior to spawning; In-Fisherman calendar period between winter and spawn.

Prey: Fish that often are eaten by other fish species.

Prop Bait: Topwater plug with one or more propellers at the front or back.

Range: Area over which a species is distributed.

Rattlebait: Hollow-bodied, sinking, lipless crankbaits that rattle loudly due to shot and slugs in the body cavity.

Reeds: Any of several species of tall, leafless emergent aquatic weeds that grow in shallow zones of lakes and reservoirs.

Reef: Rocky hump in a body of water.

Reservoir: Large man-made body of water.

Resting Spot: Location used by fish not actively feeding.

Riffle: Shallow, fast-flowing section of a stream or river.

Rig: Arrangement of components for bait fishing, including hooks, leader, sinker, swivel, beads.

Riprap: Large rocks placed along a bank.

Riverine: Having characteristics of a river.

Run: Straight, moderate-depth section of a stream or river with little depth change.

School: Group of fish of one species that move in unison.

Selective Harvest: Deciding to release or harvest fish, based on species, size, and relative abundance.

Sensory Organ: Biological system involved in sight, hearing, taste, smell, touch, or lateral line sense.

Set Rig: Rig that's cast into position on the bottom to await a strike.

Shot: Small, round sinkers pinched onto fishing line.

Silt: Fine sediment on the bottom of a body of water.

Sinkers: Variously shaped pieces of lead used to sink bait or lures.

Slip Float: Float with hole for sliding freely on line.

Slip Sinker: Sinker with a hole for sliding freely on line.

Slop: Dense aquatic vegetation matted on the surface.

Slough: Cove or backwater on a reservoir or river.

Slow Roll: Spinnerbait presentation in which the lure is retrieved slowly through and over cover objects.

Snag: Brush or tree in a stream or river.

Solitary: Occupying habitat without close association to other animals.

Sonar: Electronic fishing aid that emits sound waves underwater and interprets them to depict underwater objects.

Spawn: Reproduction of fish; In-Fisherman calendar period associated with that activity.

Species: Group of potentially interbreeding organisms.

Spine: Stiff, sharp segment of fin.

Spoon: Any of a variety of metal, plastic, or wood lures with a generally spoonlike shape and a single hook.

Sportfish: Fish species pursued by anglers.

Stock: Place fish in a body of water; population of animals.

Stress: State of physiological imbalance caused by disturbing environmental factors.

Strike: Biting motion of a fish.

Strike Window (Zone): Conceptual area in front of a fish within which it will strike food items or lures.

Structure: Changes in the shape of the bottom of lakes, rivers, or impoundments, especially those that influence fish behavior.

Stumpfield: Area of an impoundment where stands of timber have been cut prior to impoundment, leaving stumps below the surface.

Substrate: Type of bottom in a body of water.

Suspended Fish: Fish in open water hovering considerably above bottom.

Swim (Gas) Bladder: Organ of most bony fish that holds a volume of gas to make them neutrally buoyant at variable depths.

Tailwater: Area immediately downstream from a dam.

Temperature Tolerant: Able to function in a range of temperatures.

Terminal Tackle: Components of bait fishing system including hooks, sinkers, swivels, and leaders.

Thermocline: Layer of water with abrupt change in temperature, occurring between warm surface layer and cold bottom layer.

Topwaters: Lures designed to be worked on the surface.

Tracking: Following radio-tagged or sonic-tagged animals.

Trailer: A plastic skirt, grub, pork rind, livebait, or other attractor attached to a lure to entice fish.

Trailer Hook: An extra hook attached to a lure's rear hook to catch fish that strike behind the lure.

Transducer: Electronic part of a sonar unit that receives sound impulses and converts them to visual images.

Tributary: Stream or river flowing into a larger river.

Trigger: Characteristics of a lure or bait presentation that elicit a biting response in fish.

Trolling: Fishing method in which lures or baits are pulled by a boat.

Trolling Motor: Electric motor positioned on the bow or transom to push or pull the boat.

Turbid: Murky water, discolored by suspended sediment.

Turbulence: Water disturbed by strong currents.

Waterdog: Immature salamander possessing external gills.

Watershed: The region draining runoff into a body of water.

Weed: Aquatic plant.

Weedline (Weededge): Abrupt edge of a weedbed caused by a change in depth, bottom type, or other factor.

Wing Dam: Man-made earth or rock ridge to deflect current.

Winterkill: Fish mortality due to oxygen depletion under ice in late winter.

GOOD FISHING TO YOU FROM YOUR FRIENDS AT IN-FISHERMAN!

The In-Fisherman Secrets Series presents inside information on a range of fishing topics.

For more information about freshwater fishing, In-Fisherman also offers books and videos that detail fishing tactics for largemouth bass, smallmouth bass, walleye, northern pike, muskie, catfish, crappies, and other panfish, plus trout. Ice fishing's covered too. And many more select topics.

We're just a bunch of crazy fishheads who love it all and want to help you catch more fish and have more fun. For more information, call 218/829-1648, or visit our Web site <www.in-fisherman.com>.